HILARIOUS HOLIDAY HUMOR

JOKES FOR Thanksgiving

BY JANE R. DAVIS

Gareth Stevens PUBLISHING

Please visit our website, www.garethstevens.com. For a free color catalog of all our high-quality books, call toll free 1-800-542-2595 or fax 1-877-542-2596.

Library of Congress Cataloging-in-Publication Data
Names: Davis, Jane R., author.
Title: Jokes for Thanksgiving / Jane R. Davis.
Description: Buffalo, New York : Gareth Stevens Publishing, 2026. | Series: Hilarious holiday humor | Includes index. | Audience: Grades 2-3
Identifiers: LCCN 2024058677 (print) | LCCN 2024058678 (ebook) | ISBN 9781482472028 (library binding) | ISBN 9781482472011 (paperback) | ISBN 9781482472035 (ebook)
Subjects: LCSH: Thanksgiving Day–Juvenile humor. | Wit and humor, Juvenile. | LCGFT: Humor.
Classification: LCC PN6231.T566 D38 2026 (print) | LCC PN6231.T566 (ebook) | DDC 818/.602–dc23/eng/20241209
LC record available at https://lccn.loc.gov/2024058677
LC ebook record available at https://lccn.loc.gov/2024058678

Published in 2026 by
Gareth Stevens Publishing
2544 Clinton Street
Buffalo, NY 14224

Designer: Leslie Taylor
Editor: Kristen Rajczak Nelson

Photo credits: Cover (cartoons) Julia Anisimova/Shutterstock.com; series art (font) TortugaStudios/Shutterstock.com, (laughing emojis) Setia Abadi Art/Shutterstock.com, (shapes) Kseniia Belka/Shutterstock.com; p. 5 Drazen Zigic/Shutterstock.com, (inset) Chicago Bears Football Club, 1954/File:Bears-Lions-program-541212.jpg_commons.wikimedia.org; p. 6 Larry-Rains/Shutterstock.com; p. 7 Lucinda Jayne/Shutterstock.com; p. 8, 10, 16 AI generated image/Shutterstock.com; p. 9 Natalia Davidovich/Shutterstock.com; p. 11 The White House/File:P112515PS-0756 (23609234444).jpg_commons.wikimedia.org; p. 12 Bochkarev Photography/Shutterstock.com; p. 13 Elena Veselova/Shutterstock.com; p. 14 Boontoom Sae-Kor/Shutterstock.com; p. 15 PeopleImages.com - Yuri A/Shutterstock.com; p. 17 Jennie Augusta Brownscombe/File:Thanksgiving-Brownscombe.jpg_commons.wikimedia.org; p. 18 Rawpixel.com/Shutterstock.com; p. 19 Alexander Raths/Shutterstock.com, (inset) Brent Hofacker/Shutterstock.com; p. 20 Olga Lyubkin/Shutterstock.com; p. 21 Yuganov Konstantin/Shutterstock.com.

Printed in the United States of America

CPSIA compliance information: Batch #CSGS26: For further information contact Gareth Stevens at 1-800-542-2595.

CONTENTS

BOLDFACE WORDS APPEAR IN THE GLOSSARY.

Time to Eat!

Thanksgiving **celebrations** are joyful times to get together with your family! Do you or your family members travel long distances for the big meal? Have you helped bake pies or **baste** the turkey? Maybe you like to watch one of the many football games that happen on Thanksgiving Day in the United States!

Many people like to share what they are grateful, or thankful, for when sitting around the Thanksgiving table. This year, remember a few Thanksgiving jokes and make your family thankful for laughter!

Turkey, cranberries, stuffing, and pumpkin pie are **traditionally** served at Thanksgiving dinner. What does your family eat?

Thanksgiving Day football game program, 1954

LET'S CELEBRATE!

The first National Football League (NFL) game played on Thanksgiving Day happened in Detroit, Michigan, in 1934. The Detroit Lions beat the Chicago Bears!

TURKEY TALK

What month is a turkey's favorite?

Any other than November!

Did the turkey win the fight?

No, he got the stuffing knocked out of him!

What do you call a turkey on the run?

Fast food!

Wild turkeys are native to North America.

LET'S CELEBRATE!

In the United States, Thanksgiving is celebrated on the fourth Thursday in November.

How do you stuff a turkey?

Feed it a huge ice cream sundae!

What does a turkey use to find facts online?

Google, Google.

Which side of a turkey has the most feathers?

The outside.

What position does a turkey play on a baseball team?

First baste.

Turkeys are birds called fowl. Fowl are from a group of birds long kept for their eggs or meat.

How did the injured turkey get around?
He wobble, wobbled
Why did the kids invite the turkey to join their band?
He already had his own drumsticks.
A turkey met the president. What did it say?
"Pardon me."
How do turkeys like to travel best?
They take the gravy train.

A pardon is excusing someone from **punishment**. The U.S. president gives a pardon to a turkey each Thanksgiving season, letting it live and not become dinner!

President Barack Obama

LET'S CELEBRATE!

Turkeys have long been given as gifts to the U.S. president.

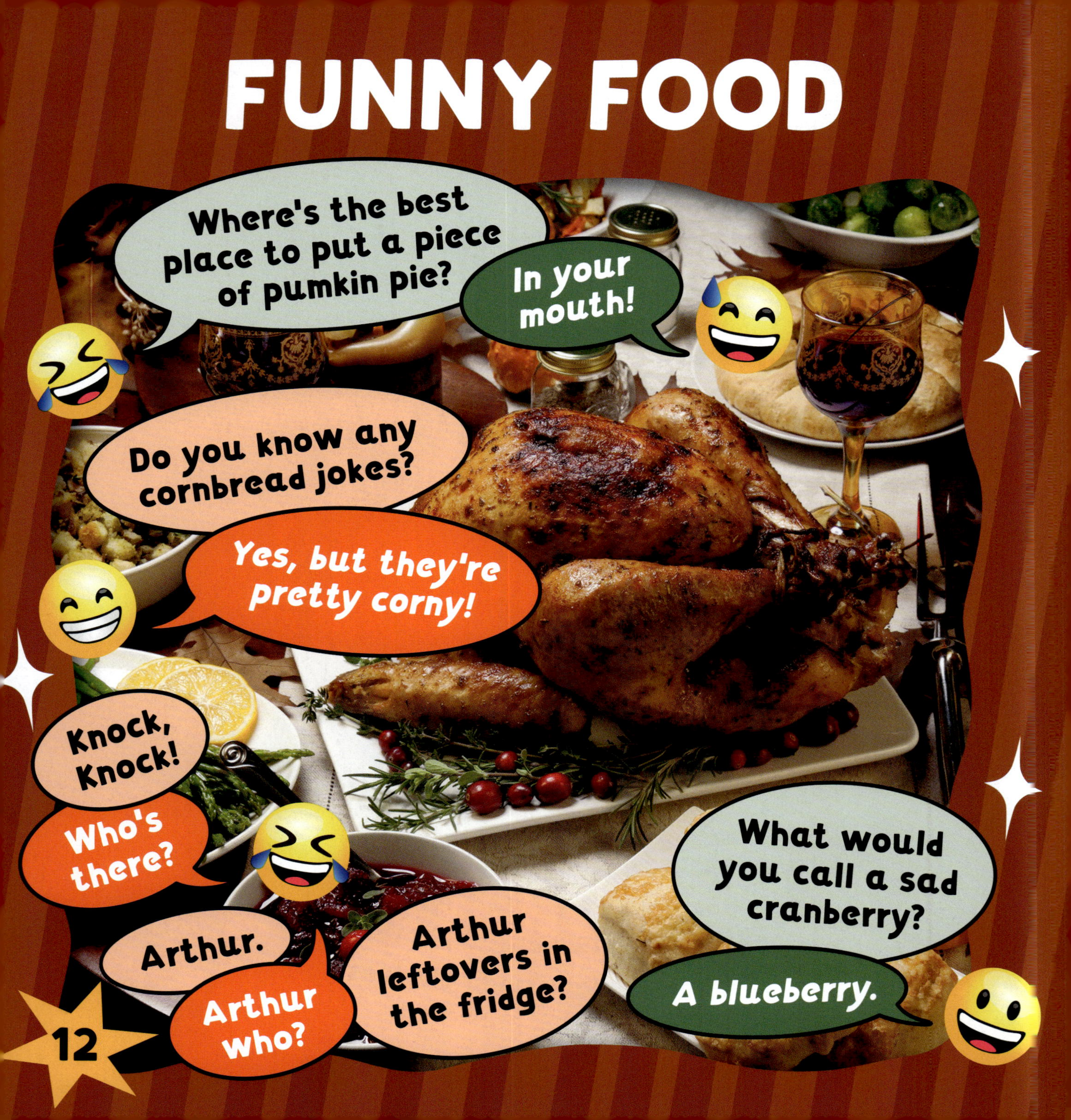

FUNNY FOOD

Where's the best place to put a piece of pumkin pie?

In your mouth!

Do you know any cornbread jokes?

Yes, but they're pretty corny!

Knock, Knock!

Who's there?

Arthur.

Arthur who?

Arthur leftovers in the fridge?

What would you call a sad cranberry?

A blueberry.

LET'S CELEBRATE!

Not every Thanksgiving pie is sweet! In some parts of the United States, people enjoy **savory** pies like tamale pie!

Pumpkin pies of many kinds have been made in North America for hundreds of years!

What's the best way to fix a pumpkin pie?

A pumpkin patch.

Why wasn't the turkey cooked all the way?

The cook didn't have enough thyme to make dinner.

What did the Christmas ham say when it met the Thanksgiving turkey?

"I've always wanted to meat you!"

thyme

Knock, Knock!

Who's there?

Don.

Don who?

Don't you dare eat all the mashed potatoes! I want some!

It takes a long time to cook a turkey! To cook an unstuffed 18-pound (8.1 kg) turkey, it takes 3 1/2 to 4 hours!

HISTORICAL HILARITY

What dance did the Pilgrims like to do?

The turkey trot.

Why wouldn't the Pilgrim make bread for Thanksgiving?

It was a crumb-y job.

What's a Pilgrim's favorite music?

Plymouth Rock.

What do you need for Thanksgiving s'mores?

Chocolate, marshmallows, and Pil-grahams.

LET'S CELEBRATE!

Turkey was probably not served at the first Thanksgiving! The fowl they ate was likely duck or goose.

Settlers of what is now Plymouth, Massachusetts, and nearby Native Americans, the Wampanoag, gathered in 1621 to celebrate a good harvest. This feast has become known as the first Thanksgiving.

SAY IT SILLY

What is a rainy Thanksgiving?

A day of fowl weather.

Knock, Knock!

Who's there?

Tamara.

Tamara who?

Tamara I'm gonna eat lots of leftovers!

What can you always expect at the end of Thanksgiving?

The letter g.

Does your family make stuffing or dressing? These dishes commonly have similar **ingredients** like bread, celery, and herbs. Stuffing is cooked inside the turkey. Dressing is cooked in a pan on its own. In some places these words mean the same thing though!

My mom tried a new recipe this Thanksgiving.

She's a real pie-oneer.

What did the salt and pepper say as the Thanksgiving guests arrived?

"Seasonings greetings!"

What should I wear to Thanksgiving dinner?

Put on a har-vest.

Where is Christmas always before Thanksgiving?

In the encyclopedia.

No matter what's on your table, being with those you love on Thanksgiving is nothing to joke about!

LET'S CELEBRATE!

The day after Thanksgiving is known as Black Friday. Many people do their Christmas shopping this day!

GLOSSARY

baste: To add liquids to food, such as meat, as it cooks.

celebration: A time to show happiness for an event through activities such as eating or playing music.

expect: To think that something is likely to happen.

ingredient: A food that is mixed with other foods.

injured: Hurt.

Pilgrim: An English colonist settling at Plymouth in 1620.

punishment: Something that makes someone suffer for wrongdoing, like a fine.

recipe: An explanation on how to make food.

savory: Flavorful without sweetness.

traditionally: Having to do with long-practiced customs.

FOR MORE INFORMATION

Books

Mavrikis, Peter. *The First Thanksgiving: Separating Fact From Fiction*. Mankato, MN: Capstone Press, 2022.

Morgan, Elizabeth and Elaine Landau. *Celebrating Thanksgiving*. Buffalo, NY: Cavendish Square Publishing, 2023.

Websites

First Thanksgiving
https://kids.nationalgeographic.com/history/article/first-thanksgiving
Read more about the history of Thanksgiving here.

162 Funny Jokes for Kids
https://www.today.com/parents/family/jokes-for-kids-rcna49138
Make your friends and family laugh with these jokes!

Publisher's note to educators and parents: Our editors have carefully reviewed these websites to ensure that they are suitable for students. Many websites change frequently, however, and we cannot guarantee that a site's future contents will continue to meet our high standards of quality and educational value. Be advised that students should be closely supervised whenever they access the internet.

INDEX